Mindful

Easy Tips and Meditations to Unleash Your Creativity and Purpose

by Karen Daniels

The obligatory legal stuff

ISBN-13: 978-1467933131

ISBN-10: 1467933139

For more information and conversations about creativity, writing online and blogging, go to my blog zencopy.com or visit karendaniels.com.

Thank you.

*A hunch is creativity
trying to tell you something.*

Frank Capra

by the author of

Your Creativity: From Ordinary to Extraordinary

http://www.karendaniels.com/KarenDaniels_Books.html

What readers are saying about

Your Creativity: From Ordinary to Extraordinary -

5 out of 5 stars! Excellent resource for parents/teachers from E. Littrell (SF Bay Area). As a parent of two gifted boys, and a 27-year veteran of gifted education, this book was refreshing and an easy-to-read reminder of some of the strategies for supporting and nurturing creativity. Written from a parent perspective from a professional in the field (Masters' Degree in Gifted Education), this book starts as a "quick read" for immediate ideas, then compels us to come back for review and reflection.

5.0 out of 5 stars! Well done! from Daniel E. Nelson. Great, easy to understand and instantly useful. Good examples; I'll use it in my classroom...Highly Recommended.

Contents

I am not afraid...

I was born to do this.

Joan of Arc

Introduction

Have you ever wondered what brings on creative enlightenment? Perhaps the result of one major life event that blows your mind, makes you sit up and say "WOW!"?

That would be great, though probably it's more subtle than that. Creative enlightenment more likely comes from a series of small steps taken within one's daily living.

As human beings living in this time and place we have the option of making creative choices all the time. We can choose to respond creatively to all those "little" things in life, and to those "big" things we consider to be life changing. But the reality is that all moments are life changing; even those we think of as unimportant because without that specific moment in time we would be different in the next moment.

This ancient Zen story speaks to the power of small moments:

There were two old masters sitting side by side. One of them reached for a needle and began to mend some clothes.

"What are you doing?" Dongshan asked.

"I'm mending clothes."

"How do you do that?"

"One stitch is like the next," said Shenshan.

"What, after twenty years of practice – that's all you can say?" said Dongshan

Shenshan put down his needle and turned to his companion. "Well then tell me. How do you sew?"

"As though the entire earth were spewing flames," said Dongshan.

Your life can be filled with moments where each one is like the next where you make the same choices you've made before, or you can choose to live a vibrant life full of flames and color and creative living.

But how do you get that vibrant life? What can you do to strive toward your best creative self and get to the core of what is unique to you so you can live the life you weren't meant to live? To begin you can take the steps that are in this book.

What you will find in this book:

Part I. What's stopping you?

How to understand and deal with the real issues and fears surrounding creativity

Part 2. Unleash your Creativity

Slow down and take a journey to the core of your creative being with these tips and meditations

Part 3: Explore Your Life Purpose

Tips to jumpstart the rest of your life

The simple and effective tips, ideas, and meditations in this book are designed to move you past your excuses, to put you in touch with your creative energy, and to help you begin to develop mindful creativity so you can aim to get the most from life.

What is Mindful Creativity?

Mindful creativity as used for the purposes of this book means consciously and consistently choosing to use your creativity to enhance your life and the lives of those around you.

PART I

What's stopping you?

How to understand and deal with the real issues and fears surrounding creativity

Is Creativity Really Worth It?

Creativity is not about creating art—though art can be part of creativity. Creativity is about original thinking and ideas and about producing something useful and original for yourself. Creativity is about groundbreaking leadership and controlling your own destiny because you don't have to follow all those who came before. Creativity is about being completely and uniquely, YOU.

Creativity is a vital skill that helps us come up with solutions—personally, professionally, and globally. We need creative thinking skills to use alongside our critical thinking skills if we are going to maximize life's opportunities. Taking the time to explore and develop your creativity will expand your problem-solving skills and give you a better sense of who you are and help you to understand your place in the universe.

With the increase of global communication the opportunity for individual creative success has never been greater. But at the very time when creativity should be one of the most important skills we can develop, according to a Newsweek article creativity in America is declining. The article states:

"The potential consequences are sweeping. The necessity of human ingenuity is undisputed. A recent IBM poll of 1,500 CEOs identified creativity as the No. 1 "leadership competency" of the future. Yet it's not just about sustaining our nation's economic growth. All around us are matters of national and international importance that are crying out for creative solutions, from saving the Gulf of Mexico to bringing peace to Afghanistan to delivering health care. Such solutions emerge from a healthy marketplace of ideas, sustained by a populace constantly contributing original ideas and receptive to the ideas of others."

If you doubt the importance of digging into yourself to expand your creativity and what you might be able to contribute to the world, let's take a trip through time by considering the power of the following ideas. These are ideas that when put forth changed all of us profoundly. Think about what the world would be like if these creative ideas had never been:

The Ancient World

Prehistoric man imagines a world inhabited by spirits

Geometry – the idea of ideal forms existing outside the physical world

Mankind envisions life after death

The week gets 7 days (ancient Egyptians had a 10 day week)

People learn to rule themselves (rather than kings etc.)

Buddhism and enlightenment

Law of cause and effect

World composed of atoms

Socrates and the pursuit of truth (btw, he never produced a single book)

Aristotle and deductive logic

Skeptics – if it possible to know anything with certainty?

The Middle Ages

Free will

Mathematicians and the power of 0

Writ of habeas corpus – must show why a prisoner's liberty is being denied

Verdicts should be settled by panel of fellow citizens

Mysticism, a direct route to God

The Renaissance

Humanism makes man "the measure of all things"

Humans aspire to an ideal world, utopia

Copernicus, the Earth revolves around the sun

The Age of Enlightenment

The scientific method

Francis Bacon, inductive reasoning

Descartes, "I think, therefore I am."

Newton, rules of the physical universe

Vico's theory of knowledge, that it comes from sense experience and beliefs

Rousseau, man is corrupted by civilization

Capitalism

Mary Wollstonecraft, womens' rights

All men are created equal

Modern Times

Transcendentalism

Genetics

Evolution

Theory of relativity

The big bang

Chaos theory

Behaviorism

Animal rights

You're probably thinking, well sure, but I'm no B.F. Skinner coming up with the idea of behaviorism. I'm no genius! Really? Well, here's your first...

Mindful Creativity Newsflash!

You don't have to be a creative genius for creativity to work for you. All of us, old or young, in heart or body, have profound levels of creativity within us.

And no matter where you believe you lie on the creativity scale at this moment in time, your creativity can be improved upon, expanded, and brought into your mindful awareness so you can make it work for you. Somewhere, hidden within you, are creative gems that have the potential to help all of us, to change your life, and the world as we know it. So, let's get going!

What's Blocking Your Creativity?

Did you ever have one of those days (weeks or even years) when you wished you could just stop having that damn desire to "be creative?" Wouldn't it be great if you could flip a switch and just do things without that constant niggling urge that pushes you to always want to do more, be more…argh! I mean, isn't it okay to just coast sometimes? To not be creative?

Have you ever considered why you might wish to be not creative? There are, in fact, good reasons why you might feel you'd be better off without a lingering creative streak. Feeling as if you'd like to get rid of the creative urge is not your fault because everything around you is conspiring to bring your creativity down a notch; truly it's no wonder creativity can feel more like a curse than a blessing.

Did you know that studies in the United States show that creativity (fantasy and imagination) actually drops when children enter Kindergarten? Think about this for a moment. Kids at Kindergarten age (5ish) are fiery balls of creativity. So why then, does this happen? Well, formal education is often a child's first venture that demands conformity.

And chances are good that you were once a child who went to Kindergarten, or the equivalent stage of education within your system. Right then and there you began to learn to suppress your creative individuality in order to do what was expected of you to fit in. And surprise surprise—you have been battling against the conformity tide ever since.

No wonder you might wish your creativity would just go away!

And even if you somehow escaped the creative squelching from formal education, social structures around the world are not highly supportive of creativity. Many cultural, social, and emotional things can interfere with your creativity. Here are a few examples inspired by Gary A. Davis:

-Businesses want to avoid expenditures that do not give immediate payback

-Societies have an emphasis on external rewards, rather than internal

-It's uncomfortable to be different

-Traditional roles and stereotypes in any culture can limit creativity

-We must be practical, right?

-Cooperation or competition can stifle creativity

-Societies desire to protect status quo

-Societies ask for obedience, duty, and conformity

-We are afraid

-We have a need to belong

-What will your parents think?

-Creativity is not in the budget

-We've never done that before

-Let's wait and see

-Walk, don't run

Frankly, anti-creative sentiment is everywhere around you. And, unless you're a hermit in a cave on top of an unclimbable mountain, anti-creativity is bound to seep into you and impact how you feel about your creative self.

When you bury your creativity for a long enough period of time you can forget it's even there. That's why it's important to take the time to understand how social, cultural, and emotional blocks are affecting you personally so you can make conscious decisions rather than unconscious ones. To help you expand your consciousness along these lines, here is my version of a Gary Davis creativity exercise. Conscious thinking about your creativity in this way is a good warm up before you dive into the meditations and mission building steps that follow.

Activities
to Develop Creative Consciousness

1. How do the following areas depress or ignite your creativity? Write a bit for each category to help you understand yourself better.

-How do the habits you've learned over the years affect your creativity?

-How do your rules, your families' rules, and societal rules, limit your creativity?

-How do you think about your creativity as part of you?

-How do your loved ones think about creativity?

-When you think about creativity, what emotions do you feel?

-Can you see things in your culture that limit your creativity?

-How does being a woman or a man limit or help your creativity?

2. Now list 5 absolutely ridiculous things that limit your creativity.

Take a look at your "ridiculous" list and ask yourself why you think you are influenced by the things that you allow to limit you. Try as we might, we can never totally unhinge ourselves from the society we live in, or completely divorce ourselves from caring, at least a little, of what the people around us think. But limiting our creativity is never the answer. And what if you want to be more creative, or even *need* to be more creative, but you just feel all gunked up with these creativity-stopping layers?

Dump Your Excuses and Get Honest

You can, with the steps in this book, start eliminating those creativity-stopping layers. As we've discussed, on a day-to day basis, society does not support highly creative people because personal creativity equals nonconformity. And because we are products of our not-particularly-supportive cultures, step one is to get a little more honest about your own creativity and the factors in your life that you've allowed to influence your ability to make creative choices.

Mindful Creativity Newsflash!

You need to stand up and claim the truth that avoiding your creativity is not about time or money or talent—or whatever excuse you have in your mind. Because it's never truly about those things. It's about fear.

The reason you need to admit the truth that it's fear, which influences us all, is simply to bring it to your conscious awareness – nothing more, nothing less. If you don't own it, you can't change it.

In mindfully becoming more honest it might help for you to understand what I call your *personal creative-avoidance dance*. I first wrote about this on my blog in a post titled What Noble Excuse Have You Designed to Fool Your Creative Self? In this post I give a few examples of the elaborate things we do to create excuses for ourselves.

First you have…

The Adventurer

If you're a foolish adventurer you start down one creative path only to "realize" that in order to get to the end of that path you must first complete something else...hours later you've done tons but not what you set out to deliver. Example: You start to design your new business card then realize it's going to have your web address so you need to redesign your home page...and rewrite your about information and....time runs out.

The Selfless Do-Gooder

If you're a foolish selfless do-gooder you devote yourself to taking care of your kids, your aging parent, or your sad friend. Yes, of course, we all have to and want to do this when it's needed. BUT, if you find yourself ALWAYS taking care of others at the expense of your creative output and fulfillment, then you must take pause and question whether you're this way because it's easier than actually facing your creativity.

The Perfect Creator

If you're a foolish perfect creator then you probably produce creative and innovative ideas and things up to a certain point. And then you tinker, tinker, tinker, redesign, redesign, redesign, rewrite, rewrite, rewrite. But you never actually deliver a final product because it's never "as good as it could be."

The Smooth Sailor

Smooth sailing, that's what you like. Fully pursuing your creative endeavors would challenge those around you, maybe even upset them and, of course, we can't have that. I mean, it's not worth upsetting your spouse just to "dabble" creatively, right?

One of these types may ring true to you. Or, you may have another avoidance dance which has served you. When you begin to understand the elaborate system you've constructed in order to avoid the fear of diving into your full potential, then you have a chance of stopping the sequence of events – you can keep yourself on track and actually get your business done.

Now I ask you, what personal psychological dance have you designed to fool your creative self?

In the process of self-dissection, don't be too hard on yourself. It's important to understand that your excuses stem from what you feel is self-preservation. By the time most of us reach adulthood, fitting in and not rocking the boat has become so ingrained we don't even pause to think about it.

So, what can you do to change your creative-avoidance pattern so that you can get closer to living more fully with your authentic creative self?

5 Strategies
to Get You Out of Excuse Mode

1. Suck it up

As they say, feel the fear and do it anyway. Quit belly aching and worrying about fitting in or being loved by your spouse or best friend, or having enough money or time. Do what you were put on this Earth to do; reach into your raw self and share your creative gifts with us. The world needs them!

2. Distract Yourself

Perception is reality. You may find that certain creative tasks don't trigger your fears and therefore your avoidance dancing, while other seemingly small tasks drive you to suddenly "have to do something else." The good news is, you can distract yourself. Once you develop awareness of which tasks or ideas or creative thoughts trigger the start of your avoidance, you can come up with other reasons why you need to do those tasks. For example:

Don't think, "I need to get my website up so I can sell my artwork (and be vulnerable and ostracized)."

Think, "I'm going to work on my website so I'll know how to use that design template program so I can help my kids do their own websites." This way, the fact that you get your own website up and running becomes incidental.

3. The Work Around

Swap fear tasks with a friend. One person's fear is another person's easy task. Let's suppose the idea of creating business cards triggers the avoidance dance. Months after knowing you need to do this, you've still made no headway with actually having a completed card. Track down one of your buddies who did a great business card for themselves, (because for them it's a no fear task), find out which task they are stuck on (that is an easy one for you), and then swap tasks. They do your card, you put together their photo book. Win win. Though the workaround does not force you to deal with some of your issues, using it will allow you to start getting more of your creative tasks done which in and of itself will kick start your creativity.

4. Play "What if"

Contemplate something creative you want to do. Feel your feelings and play "with if" with yourself.

What if I hit the publish button on my website?

I can never go back.

What if I can never go back?

I won't be anonymous anymore.

What if I'm not anonymous anymore?

I can't hide.

What if I can't hide anymore?

I'll be vulnerable.

People will make fun.

I won't be loved.

My spouse will hate me...

he'll file for divorce and I'll lose my family and be forever alone and and and...

You get the idea. Often our fears are random nameless shadows and when we bring them to the light of day they lose their power. If you are more than 10 years of age you already know that many of the things you fear are going to happen, never actually do happen.

Playing "what if" allows you to get in touch with your real fears so you can begin to understand what's truly driving you to make your excuses. THEN you can deal with them. Playing "what if" on even one fear task will give you great insight into yourself.

5. Ask yourself this:

What's so good about fitting in anyway? Trying to be something you're not probably didn't work well for you in high school and it won't work now.

On a regular basis I have the privilege of speaking about creativity groups of teachers. Often, as I began, everyone dutifully pulls out writing utensils and paper as they adopt a serious expression and poise themselves to take notes. A profound contrast to the response you get from a gaggle of kids when you let them know they get to do something creative – yelling, jumping, spitballs, and general mayhem.

At what point in our lives does creativity stop being "fun" for us?

There's a good answer in a book titled, "Ignore Everybody And 30 Other Keys to Creativity" by Hugh MacLeod.

In Chapter 7, titled *Everyone is born creative; everyone is given a box of crayons in kindergarten,* he states:

"Then when you hit puberty they take the crayons away and replace them with dry, uninspiring books on algebra, history, etc. Being suddenly hit years later with the

"creative bug" is just a wee voice telling you, "I'd like my crayons back, please. So, you have to listen to the wee voice or it will die...taking a big chunk of you along with it. They're only crayons. You didn't fear them in kindergarten, why fear them now?"

Don't let your fears stop you from living a life of passion and mindful creativity.

Give yourself permission to figuratively bring the color of crayons back into your life. People may not like it, people may laugh, people may do their best to discourage you. But that is simply because they, too, are afraid. By developing mindful creativity for yourself and living it, you will show them by example, the way to their own creative freedom.

Now, it's time to address the next phase of developing your mindful creativity—the accumulation of energy that has come with society, fear, and all your excuses. The following meditations will help get some of the gunk out and help you get your creativity moving again, unblock you where you're stuck, and alleviate some of your creative fears.

PART 2

Unleash your Creative Energy

Slow down and take a journey to the core of your creative being with these tips and meditations

Slow down

In today's high tech societies, we have many things competing for our attention at any given moment in time; frankly it's kind of miraculous we get anything important done at all. We literally stream our distractions so they are nonstop, and for many people this can be somewhat addicting because we often get positive feedback and self validation – as in, another Twitter Follower – yippee!

To move closer to living in a mindfully creative way, you should on occasion unplug and slow down.

(Some of the following slow down and focus information is inspired by Leo Babauta, one of the world's top bloggers).

Slowing down has many benefits including:

-Better focus. When you slow down, you can focus better. It's hard to focus if you're moving too fast.

-Deeper focus. Rushing produces shallowness, because you never have time to dig beneath the surface. Slow down and dive into deeper waters.

-Better appreciation. You can really appreciate what you have, what you're doing and who you're with when you take the time to slow down and really pay attention.

-Enjoyment. When you appreciate things, you enjoy them more. Slowing down allows you to enjoy life to the fullest.

-Less stress. Rushing produces anxiety and higher stress levels. Slowing down is calmer, relaxing, peaceful.

-Slowing down and focusing on the essential allows you to get done the things that matter most.

Tips to help you Focus

-unplug

-have a disconnect time each day

-work somewhere where there is no connection

-get outside

-forget your mobile device

-use blocking software

-disconnect away from work

If you don't take the time to slow down and focus because you are too plugged in you are simply not going to get the most from your creative self and therefore your life. Some time ago when Leo Babauta gave up doing email he was simultaneously applauded and booed. Here's what Leo says about that:

"The simple act of giving up email was either hugely courageous, or arrogant, because I wasn't living up to the expectation of society that I'd be available via email and at least make the attempt to reply. Interesting, because just a decade earlier, many people didn't use email and no one cared if they didn't."

What's important is that you spend time on what matters to you *and your goals*. Bring your energies and attention into focus so you're constantly moving yourself in the direction you want to go. If you like to create, to be creative, beware that creating is a completely separate process from consuming and communicating. Consuming and communicating can aid in creating, of course, they can lay the groundwork. But at some point you need to actually sit down and create. Or stand up and create. But create.

Once you've put the idea of slowing down and focusing into your conscious awareness, it's time to take a journey to the core of your creative being to let more of your creative energy fly free. Get started with the following meditative energy tools.

A Quick Note on Meditation

Meditation in nearly any form can calm you and put you more in touch with, well – you. Meditation is a doorway into self, a tool which helps you become more aware of the energy and information which constantly surrounds you.

Mindful Creativity Newsflash!

You don't even have to "believe" in meditation or energy for these tools to work. So, whether you're a believer or a pretender, all good!

The meditations/visualizations here are designed for everyone and anyone who wishes to gain greater access to their authentic creative self; For those who are willing to put their excuses aside and are seeking ways to get their creativity flowing—and to keep it flowing. The following relaxing meditative tools can take you on an in-depth journey toward your best creative self.

While you go through these techniques one of the most important things to remember is to listen to the voice within you—that voice that lets you know what is right for you and what is wrong for you. Though I am suggesting particular methodologies I encourage you to take only the portions of these meditations that feel good to you and then discard the rest. In other words, make it your own.

Your Meditation Space

Meditation can be done standing, jogging, sailing, making love, or while doing anything else (not recommended while driving or operating heavy machinery though!). However, in the beginning I suggest sitting on a comfortable chair because you may be able to focus more easily. Many times when we need to find calm within ourselves and we most need centering, we are not seated in a comfortable chair, but talking to others or arguing with our boss. Don't hesitate to use these tools whenever you need them. All these techniques become easier the more you do them.

<u>Energy</u>

One of the great things about creative energy is that it works even though you may not be consciously aware of it. Thoughts, feelings, and words, all contain energy. When energy moves, creativity happens. So if you go through these visualizations and aren't sure anything is happening don't worry. It is. And remember, there is no one right way.

About the Meditations

1. In the beginning

A good starting point for all creative levels; includes basic tools of centering, releasing unwanted energy and bringing forth your creative energy.

2. Communication with yourself

This meditation helps open up the channels of communication between your physical self and your creative self.

3. Healing your creative space

Meditation 3 helps you to locate your more vulnerable areas and to take steps toward self-healing so you can live more creatively.

How to Use these Meditations

All the meditations begin with a series of quick cues. These are followed by text which elaborates on the cues. I suggest that you read the text first to become familiar with the ideas and words. Then, when you're ready to meditate use the quick cues to walk yourself through. If this is your first time going through the meditations I recommend you start with the first one to become familiar with the terms. However, ultimately it is not necessary to do these meditations in any particular order.

Meditation 1
In the beginning...

Quick Cues

Private room (Center of your head)

Personal grounding cord

Outward flow (Releasing unwanted energy)

Golden Sun (Getting your creative energy back)

Private room. Center of your head

Shut your eyes and picture a room in the center of your head. Design the room to your tastes, no one else's. Make it a comfortable place for you to be. Perhaps you want a place to sit. Or not. You can put as much or as little detail in this room as you desire. The bottom line is making the room whatever you want it to be. After you have completed this room imagine yourself in the room. Walk around, sit, sing, or just be. Feel how it feels to be in a place of your own creation.

Personal grounding cord

Now while you are in your room, imagine a cord connecting the base of your spine to the center of the earth; just assume that the cord goes there. This cord can be made of light, water, chain, ballpoint pens, slinkies, tree trunks, whatever. Anything you like at the moment. This is *your* grounding cord. Your grounding cord is going to work for you like a lightning rod; allowing you to release unwanted energy.

Releasing unwanted energy

Now, as you picture yourself in the center of your head (a mini-you) assume that you have unwanted (not yours) energy somewhere in your space.

Now, from the center of your head tell yourself that you are going to release any unwanted energy down your grounding cord.

Just by thinking, imagining, or wanting it to happen, energy will flow.

Golden Sun. Calling back your energy

Now as this energy flows from your space you need to bring back your own energy. Keep visualizing that you are in your private room. Then imagine that above the top of your head there is a big golden ball forming that is made of your own energy. This is energy that you have unintentionally placed elsewhere. Your energy will keep coming into the ball and the ball will get bigger and bigger creating a large golden sun of your own essence.

Basking in sunlight. Reclaim your energy

When you are ready, allow the sun to come down onto the top of your head and let the energy in this ball flow into and bathe you/your body. Tell the energy to go into the places where you need it most. You don't have to know where these areas are, just be certain that it will work. Repeat the golden sun tool as much as you want to replenish yourself with your own creative energy. Bask in the warmth of your own energy.

You now know how to 'be' in the center of your head and ground yourself. These two tools together are called centering.

Meditation 2
Communication with Self

Quick Cues

Center yourself

Points of communication

Talk to yourself

Listen to yourself

Reclaim your energy

Center yourself

As explained in the first meditation *In The Beginning*, bring yourself into the center of your head and be in your private room. Once there, create your grounding cord. Something which pleases you at this moment on this day. Tell your grounding cord it will work for you by draining off unwanted energy.

Points of Communication

Some of the specific points from which you can communicate with yourself are in your throat and heart areas. While you are still visualizing yourself in your room in the center of your head, imagine that the energies in your throat and heart areas are getting brighter. You may or may not perceive colors, feelings, or sensations. Whatever your experience it's right for you. Within this energy that has gotten brighter, there are areas where you will be able to communicate clearly with yourself. Allow these points to become brighter still. If you don't get a sense of where these points are, pretend.

Talk to yourself

Stay in the center of your head as much as is possible. From there, say hello to these very bright points of light. You may or may not sense that you get an answer back from your body. In either case, continue on.

Now, decide what you want to communicate to yourself, to these bright points and just say it or think it. An I love you to self is always good. Bring up anything that you want these points to know. Let yourself know that you are interested in amping up your creative energy. Tell yourself a joke.

Listen to yourself

Now, ask these bright points if they have anything to communicate to you. Be still and listen. Do you imagine thoughts at that moment? That's communication from you, for you. If you perceive nothing, again, that's dandy too. The more you do this, the more aware you will become. Do the colors change? Just try and be aware of anything at all and accept that as a communication.

Be with yourself for as long as is comfortable and just feel how it feels to be you and in communication with yourself. Enjoy your creative energy and power.

Reclaim your energy. As discussed in the Beginning meditation, allow a golden sun of your own energy to form above your head. Bring the sun into your space and allow it to fill your body and self, paying particular attention to your heart and throat areas.

You now know, in addition to centering, one way to communicate with yourself.

Meditation 3
Healing Your Creative Space

Quick Cues

Center yourself

Adjusting your energy

Find and release unwanted energy

Replenish

Center yourself

As explained in the first meditation, be in your private room. Create your grounding cord by using something that makes you smile or laugh. Tell your grounding cord to drain off unwanted energy.

Adjusting your energy

Imagine or pretend that you have energy that is within and around you. Generally speaking, for everyday wear, the outer edge of your energy should go one to two feet from your body. If you feel tired and depleted you may be letting your energy spread out too far. Visualize that the outer edge of your energy is at the optimum distance from your body for you; to start try about 18 inches from your body. Feel how that feels. Bring it in closer and move it out further. Play with it. Have fun.

Find and release unwanted energy

While you are in your private room in your head, look around and see if there is any person or anything else there, that you did not invite or place there. You should be the only person in the center of your head. Allow unwanted energy to become brighter so you can see it. Create a door or window or slide leading out of your room. Kick out, throw, or toss out, any other people or unwanted energy. Do some room cleaning. This energy that you toss out will return to its owner so you are doing both of you a favor.

Now with your head clearer, allow any energy in your body that keeps you from healing yourself, to become known to you. It can become known to you by becoming brighter, by physical pain, by you just feeling, sensing, or knowing that it is there. As soon as you recognize some unwanted energy here are a few ways to release it from your space. Visualize that the energy is moving to, and down, your grounding cord. Or imagine from your room that you have a huge hand. Reach down to the unwanted energy and pull it from your space. Toss it onto the moon. Another way is to imagine that all this energy that does not belong in your space is connected. See it as a jumpsuit you are wearing that you want to take off. Put a zipper in the suit and unzip it. Step out of it. Allow it to be sucked down into the center of the planet. Play with these three tools. You can use one or all of them. Use whatever feels like it works best for you.

Replenish with healing energy

Allow your sun to form above your head - this time filled with creative healing energy. It can be any (or many) color which makes you feel good. Slowly lower the sun into you. Allow it to fill you up, particularly the places where you have just finished releasing unwanted energy.

Bask in your creative self.

Meditation end note

All of the previous thoughts and meditations will make you more mindfully aware of things that are standing in the way of your creativity and your creative energies. Once you've completed this part of the process you need to find a direction for yourself—to choose when and where to direct your new found creative energies.

Part 3, Explore Your Life Purpose, will help you get started on finding direction.

PART 3

Explore Your Life Purpose

Tips to jumpstart the rest of your life

Where do You Want to Go?

Now that you've acknowledged some of your fears and self-imposed limitations, and played around with your creative energies, it's time to make some decisions on where you want to go from here. You need to come up with a "plan" of sorts; but mindfully applying creativity to your life and the world in significant ways really means that you need to approach your life with more than just a plan. Seth Godin, one of the more successful creative people today, says, "There's nothing wrong with having a plan. Plans are great. But missions are better. Missions survive when plans fail, and plans almost always fail."

The secret to mindful living is balance: conscious, purposeful balance. Mindful creativity is part of mindful living. Understanding the purpose of your life will allow you to aim in desired directions, both personally and professionally. As you envision your life purpose you should get excited, feel proud, and illuminate the points where you are part of something bigger than yourself.

An important step in understanding your purpose is to actually write your life vision down. You can focus on just a few words, or have fully developed pages filled with detail. You have to do what suits you and your personality best.

To get the ball rolling, here are some short and longer vision examples from humanresources.about.com:

"To inspire, motivate, and empower people to discover their life purpose and to reach their full potential."

"My vision is to be remembered when I'm gone from this life for enjoying every day I was blessed with; impacting every person that I had the pleasure of meeting in a positive way; inspiring all to dare to make their life's work be something that is truly enjoyable and meaningful to them; motivating people to be innovative and to use the power of their creative minds; providing entertaining "stories" through daily interactions with others to help people to remember each day they had with me; helping people come to know and understand who they are and how easy it is

to become who they'd like to be. I want to be loved – especially by my family – but by as many as possible, and to be able to come to love them as well. I'd like for people to tell tales of the times that we spent together for many years after I've gone; that will be the true measure of value of my time on this earth, or whether I was just successful at avoiding death for a long time."

"To realize my vision, I must exceed the expectations of my friends, family, and readers. I will accomplish this by committing to my values and creativity, and by aiming for, and offering to others, the highest levels of creativity, spirituality, and information of which I am capable. I will maintain a focus on the value of creative freedom and the expression of that freedom which is most appropriate for each person. In this way I will help ensure that I honor my values, that what I offer is creatively innovative, and that my own growth goals are met along with the growth goals of those I come in contact with."

Your life vision is the "why" of you. If you consistently make choices, personally and professionally, that align with your personal vision, you will remain on target for your life and undoubtedly be happier than if you don't. Defining your vision by creating actual statements to help you understand your life purpose is a starting point from which you can then begin making creative choices that will keep you moving toward your ultimate purposeful goals.

Defining Your Life Vision

To help you get started defining your
creative life vision, I've extrapolated from
Franklin Covey's straightforward mission
building method. You can see the Covey's
mission building process online at
http://www.franklincovey.com/msb/. I've
modified the steps below to pertain
specifically to developing mindful
creativity.

Answer or complete the following:

1. I am at my creative best when...

2. I am at my creative worst when...

3. My favorite creative thing to do at work is...

4. My favorite creative thing to do in my personal life is...

5. Some of my natural talents and creative gifts are...

6. If I had unlimited time and resources and knew I could not fail I would use my creativity to...

7. My life's creative work includes...

8. When you are dead, what would you like said about your creative contributions?

9. Project ahead; what would you consider to be the most important future creative contribution to society?

10. What do you feel you should do or change about yourself – even if you have dismissed those things before?

11. What creative people, past or present, has most influenced you in your life – what single attribute or quality has drawn you to them or their ideas? List several.

12. What are the most important things you can do in each of the following areas that will have the greatest positive impact on

your life and help you use your creativity and achieve a sense of balance?
Physical, spiritual, mental, and social/emotional.

When you've completed the above thoughts and questions you can take your responses and put them into the following format:
I am at my creative best when (answer 1) and I will try to prevent times when (answer 2). I will increase my chances of enjoying my work by finding employment where I can (answer 3). I will find creative enjoyment in my personal life through (answer 4). I will seek to find opportunities to use my natural talents and creative gifts such as (answer 5). I can do anything I set my mind to. I will (answer 6). My life's creative work includes (answer 7). I will be a person who (answer 8). My most important future contribution to will be (answer 9). From now on I will stop procrastinating and start working on (answers to 10). I will strive to incorporate the following attributes into my life: (answers to 11). I will constantly renew myself by focusing on the four dimensions of my life: (list your responses to question 12).

Your Personal Values – Words to Live By

What do you cherish in life? What do you think and believe? Your personal strategies include the most important talents and personal traits that you can, and will, use to accomplish your mission and get ever closer to your personal vision. On the following pages you will find clouds of value words (words from Steve Pavlina's personal development for smart people) that you can use as starting points. Select up to about 50 words that feel essential to who you are; include words that will help you fulfill the statement you completed above.

Affection Altruism
Adoration Amusement Ambition
Adroitness Alertness Assertiveness
Accuracy
Adaptability Audacity
Accomplishment Articulacy
Acceptance Aggressiveness Appreciation Awareness
Abundance Anticipation
Accessibility Approachability Awe
Achievement
Activeness Availability
Adventure Attractiveness
Affluence Assurance
Agility Attentiveness
Acknowledgement

Boldness
Best Bravery
Belonging Bliss
Benevolence
Beauty Buoyancy
Balance
Brilliance

Coolness
Comfort Conviction
Cleanliness Cordiality
Carefulness Connection Creativity
Candor Cheerfulness Contribution
Certainty Completion Courage
Conformity
Calmness Compassion
Capability Charm Consciousness
Celebrity Clear-mindedness
Challenge Consistency
Charity Cleverness Contentment Cooperation Curiosity
Commitment Control
Clarity Conviviality
Chastity Confidence Congruency Correctness
Camaraderie Closeness Courtesy Continuity
Credibility
Craftiness
Cunning

62

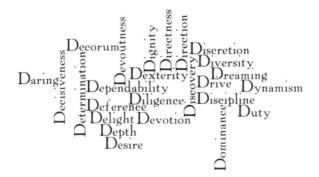

Daring Decorum Devoutness Dignity Directness Direction Discretion
Decisiveness Determination Dexterity Discovery Diversity Dreaming
Dependability Drive Dynamism
Diligence Discipline
Deference Devotion Duty
Delight
Depth Dominance
Desire

Enthusiasm Exhilaration Exuberance
Elation Energy Experience
Empathy Expertise
Economy Expectancy
Effectiveness Expediency Extravagance
Eagerness Encouragement Expressiveness
Efficiency Entertainment
Ecstasy Elegance Enjoyment
Education Excitement Exploration
Endurance
Extroversion
Excellence

Grace
Frugality Fun Giving
Fortitude Gallantry Gregariousness Gratitude
Focus Frankness Generosity Guidance
Friendliness Growth
Freedom Gentility

Humility Health Heart
Happiness Hygiene Hospitality
Holiness Honesty
Honor Helpfulness
Hopefulness
Harmony Humor Heroism

Integrity
Industry Inspiration Intuition
Impartiality Insightfulness Intuitiveness Justice
Imagination Inquisitiveness Intimacy Inventiveness
Impact Independence Intrepidness Judiciousness
Ingenuity Intelligence Investing
Intensity Introversion Joy

Keenness Logic Mastery
Love Meekness Motivation
Kindness Leadership Liberation Majesty Mellowness
Knowledge Longevity
Learning Loyalty Mysteriousness
Liberty Matter Meticulousness
Liveliness Modesty Mindfulness
Maturity

Resolve
Relaxation Rest
Refinement Resilience Restraint
Recognition Resourcefulness
Realism Religiousness Reverence
Reasonableness
Recreation Resolution Richness
Reliability
Reason Reflection Rigor
Respect

Sacredness
Silence
Silliness
Strength
Success
Support Simplicity Surprise Sharing Soundness
Satisfaction Stillness Solidarity Sensuality
Speed Spirituality Shrewdness Supremacy Solitude
Sagacity Significance Spontaneity Sanguinity Serenity
Saintliness Self-reliance Sensitivity
Sympathy Stealth Skillfulness Stability
Selflessness Sincerity
Structure Spirit
Spunk
Sexuality
Synergy
Security
Service
Self-control

Uniqueness
Timeliness Vision
Tranquility Vigor Winning Wonder
Thrift Trust Utility Vitality Wealth
Truth Victory Vivacity
Traditionalism Temperance Trustworthiness Watchfulness
Understanding Zeal Willingness
Thoughtfulness
Thoroughness Unflappability Willfulness
Transcendence Youthfulness
Thankfulness Usefulness Wittiness
Teamwork Unity Variety Warmth
Tidiness Valor Virtue Wisdom

65

Once you've selected your initial list of words that feel essential to who you are trim your list in half. And here comes the hard part. Trim your value words list in half one more time. Now put the words you have in order of importance to you. Could you apply some of these words specifically to yourself when you think about creativity? Your life? Consciously use these words to help guide your choices and behavior. If abundant is one of your words stop making choices that lead you away from an abundant life. Live your words, model them, make creative and live choices based on these words; share them and take action based on your value words.

A Note on Time

Part of your responsibility for your own life, and the reason it's important to define aspects of yourself by completing the exercises above, is that we are all working off limited resources and the limited time we have each day. Every minute you use is a minute you will never get back.

That's why:

It's important to choose what you do mindfully. When you better understand the vision you have for your life then your daily choices will lead you ever closer to your creative legacy and the abundant life you seek.

When you invest in yourself now by giving yourself the gift of consistent direction you will remain on track and be a more fulfilled person because you will remain true to your unique creativity as you live your vision.

And only when you live true to yourself and your creative gifts will you fully be offering the world your powerful personal legacy.

Pulling it all Together

The difference between those who succeed in the way they want in life, and those who do not, is direction and consistency. Barreling through life without direction and hoping that things will just happen to go your way is not an effective method to get where you want to go.

That said, there are many things that happen in life which we cannot control; factors that throw off the best laid plans. Many paths will keep your vision alive and it is your creativity, used mindfully, that will allow you to duck and dodge life's events Understanding your vision, rather than just having a plan, and then using your creativity as a means to help you adapt to whatever life throws you will help you remain true to your vision.

Final Remarks

The opportunity to use your creativity mindfully in order to help fulfill your life purpose, happens every hour of every day. As you approach your day today, or tomorrow, give yourself credit for the creative way you think, initiate, or respond to a conversation; enjoy your weekly ahas! as you contemplate your new ideas (ideas that just might change the world!). It's time to stop the excuses, focus, get in touch with your creative energy, and live fully toward fulfilling the vision you have for your life.

Mindfulness is paying attention to the present moment. Creativity as a form of mindfulness reminds us that there is possibility in all things. When we abandon ourselves to this very moment in time we begin living in a fully conscious state and develop the ability to experience life in its creative entirety.

May you have a long and healthy life lived creatively as if the entire earth were spewing flames!

Books by Karen Daniels

Creativity Books

1. Your Creativity: From Ordinary to Extraordinary
   print https://www.createspace.com/3616570
   kindle http://www.amazon.com/dp/B004Z80R4M

2. Mindful Creativity
   print https://www.createspace.com/3723368
   kindle http://www.amazon.com/dp/B006LQEFZS

IVF Books

1. IVF: The Ultimate Realty Game
   print: https://www.createspace.com/3516461
   kindle: http://www.amazon.com/dp/B004LROPMC
   all other digital formats
   https://www.smashwords.com/books/view/99510

2. Surviving In-Vitro Fertilization
   print https://www.createspace.com/3644938
   kindle: http://www.amazon.com/dp/B005F60XU6
   all other digital formats
   https://www.smashwords.com/books/view/103563

3. The Baby About to be Born
   print https://www.createspace.com/3586347
   kindle: http://www.amazon.com/dp/B004ZL9SUS

Fiction

Science Fiction/Adventure *The Zaddack Tales*
1. **Dancing Suns, Book 1**
   print https://www.createspace.com/3589033
   Kindle http://www.amazon.com/dp/B004XJ6CHY
2. **Mentor's Lair, Book 2**
   print https://www.createspace.com/3590395
   kindle http://www.amazon.com/dp/B0050D8PM2
3. **Mindspark, Book 3**
   print https://www.createspace.com/3590430
   kindle http://www.amazon.com/dp/B0050D8PXG
4. Complete Zaddack Tales Trilogy
   kindle http://www.amazon.com/dp/B0050KEEES

I'm privileged you read one of my books. Thank you!

Karen Daniels

About the Author

Karen Daniels has her M.A. in Educational Psychology and makes her living through one of her greatest creative joys—writing. About life she says, "Who knew?"

She is the author of numerous published books covering a broad range of topics from Creativity to In-vitro Fertilization, and include such titles as Your Creativity: From Ordinary to Extraordinary and In-vitro Fertilization: The Ultimate Reality Game. Fiction titles include The Zaddack Tales trilogy; Dancing Suns, Mentor's Lair, and Mindspark—an epic adventure in spiritual science fiction.

Karen is an internationally published poet, online content specialist, and creativity mentor. Her friends consider her renegade, spiritual, and a bit odd.

Connect with Karen and see all her books at http://www.karendaniels.com/ or boost your own creativity and writing skills by visiting her blog http://ZenCopy.com and getting your copy of her free creativity ebook (http://zencopy.com/free-creativity-ebook/).

Karen's websites:

- http://www.karendaniels.com
  – official site

- http://www.ivfcreation.com
  – supports IVF

- http://zencopy.com
  – creativity/writing books

- http://www.giftedresource.com
  – gifted children/education/creativity

Resources

The following resources served as inspiration and quotes for this book:

1. Unmissable Articles on Writing
http://www.writetodone.com/

2. Newsweek: The Creativity Crisis
http://www.newsweek.com/2010/07/10/the-creativity-crisis.html

3. TIME: 100 Ideas that Changed the World
http://amzn.to/vROg00

4. Zencopy: Your Write to Success
http://zencopy.com/2011/01/27/what-noble-excuse-have-you-designed-to-fool-your-creative-self/

5. Creativity is Forever by Gary A. Davis
http://amzn.to/sMXyaM

6. Ignore Everybody And 30 Other Keys to Creativity" by Hugh MacLeod
http://amzn.to/rZOT4j

7. Focus: Simplicity in the age of distractions by Leo Babauta
http://focusmanifesto.s3.amazonaws.com/FocusFree.pdf

8. Be Here Now: Mindfulness and the Creative Spirit
http://www.psychologytoday.com/blog/the-healing-arts/200902/be-here-now-mindfulness-and-the-creative-spirit

please note: amazon book links are affiliate links